Life's Magic Carousel

How to Grab the Brass Ring
Before the Music Stops

KAREN LEEDS

Life Coaching Magic

Karen Leeds, Life Coaching Magic

"You are amazing and insightful!"

"I feel relaxed and in control of my life."

"I am thinking about my life in a new way."

www.LifeCoachingMagic.com

ISBN: 978-0-9969069-0-6

Get your free ebook at

www.LifeCoachingMagic.com

(for a little life coaching magic)

"STOP **SWABBING**
SOMEONE ELSE'S DECK
AND
CAPTAIN
YOUR OWN SHIP!"

Karen Leeds
Life Coach

Dedicated to my parents, who died way too soon but instilled in me a curiosity, love of creativity, and a desire for connection — as well as a need to list only words starting with the letter "C" apparently.

CONTENTS

ACKNOWLEDGEMENTS

I want to thank Donna Kozik, leader of "Write a Book in a Weekend," for helping bring this book to fruition. I was afraid I would feel squeezed over the weekend. I didn't! (I survived lawn mowing, leaf blowing, a broken printer, and mistakenly deleting a huge section of my draft.)

I was thrilled to publish my first book, in an enjoyable group, rather than creating an 11th draft that would wallow miserably on my desk. There, it could only hope that one day it might be chosen from its dark corner to be brutally edited, and when only vaguely recognizable, perhaps to venture out into the magnificent world to find at least one compassionate reader who would rescue it and put an end to its loneliness and suffering.

Chester Goad – best book buddy during the weekend event.

Jennifer Geiger – thinker, editor, advisor, cover photo photographer, and daughter extraordinaire.

Carlos Villa – illustrator who brought my quotes to life.

Avanska Designs – colorful lettering over book cover photo.

Lisa Alpert at WebThreeSixty.com – front and back book cover text and formatting as well as website support.

Paul Scannell – fun photographs for website & blog.

Family & friends – 99Designs book cover design feedback.

Paul Gustafson – hypnosis cured my fear of public speaking.

"Never mind that it's not working for me. I've done it this way forever — changing now would be traumatic, unfamiliar, scary, different, new and hmmm, maybe that might not be such a bad thing."

— Karen Leeds

ABOUT THE AUTHOR

Karen Leeds, founder of Life Coaching Magic, helps people discover their power, so they can gain the clarity and confidence to speak up and take action for what they want. Karen locates people who are running themselves ragged — lacking time and energy for things they want in their lives. She helps them live peacefully and authentically.

She offers them a new perspective, provides them with sneaky secrets of the universe (like speaking up, setting boundaries, and living in the moment), carefully removes any impulsive temptation to volunteer their energies to random passersby, prevents them from wallowing in guilt or anger, and lovingly sends them out into the world confident and ready for anything.

Clients/readers may find that person they long to date, feel empowered at work, create rewarding friendships, set boundaries with well-meaning relatives, cross "zip-line experience in Mexico" off their bucket list, enjoy down time at a play, go for leisurely walks with the neglected doggie, and, above all, spend time lazily soaking in a tub, reading that new novel everyone is buzzing about. (Oh wait — that described my life!)

Clients discover they are suddenly filled with a new power and zest for living that has now morphed into a desirable, extraordinary life, and practically overnight.

Karen has written 13 articles for *Good Men Project* about what it means to be a good man today. (Frankly, these apply to women too.) They can be read at goodmenproject.com by typing in KAREN LEEDS.

Karen is featured in Boston Voyager Magazine (online). The article can be viewed by going to BostonVoyager.com and typing in KAREN LEEDS.

Karen has published several short stories:

- "My Fearless Five-Year-Old Self" in a collection of 42 short stories called "If Only I Knew Then What I Know Now." (Karen feels like she has spent the rest of her life trying to get back to who she was at age 5.)

- "My Suddenly Grateful Self" in a collection called "I Can Feel the Love." (It was inspired by both the Andover/North Lawrence gas explosions and Karen's parents' deaths 4 months apart. Karen discovered there is always a silver lining in whatever happens.)

- "Ferret Shenanigans or Simply Odd?" in Donna Kozik's collection of stories called "Pawsome Friends." (It is about Karen's daughter's ferret, Georgie — possibly an oddball, though he was the only ferret she has known.)

- "One Incredibly Free-Wheeling Woman" in Donna Kozik's collection of stories called "The Gratitude Project." (Karen's discovery that she had freedom once there was no longer a boyfriend, child or pet at home.)

INTRODUCTION

This is intended to be a "LIFE COACH IN A BOOK" for anyone who wants to make small changes in life like tuning in to what you want and deciding to stop putting others first.

I added fun quotes and illustrations to this short book so that readers might experience it as light-hearted and entertaining. I wanted someone with a short attention span to keep reading. I also hoped that a teenager might find it engaging so they could make a difference with their whole life still ahead of them.

Now, you don't really need to work with a life coach. (*Hope those other life coaches don't come after me.*) This book offers a path for you to trade up your current seat (or bench) on life's carousel to one that is more of a "winning" seat. (In case you're not familiar with the concept mentioned in the subtitle, on a merry-go-round (or carousel) there was often a brass ring. The goal was to grab the ring before the ride and music stopped. Then you would win another ride. For this book, it is intended to convey the idea that grabbing the brass ring means winning or having a great life.) I am here to tell you that YOU can have the LIFE you were DESTINED to live.

This book is sneaky. It is designed to be simple and elegant and make you laugh, so you keep reading, while secretly causing you to make changes in your life that create momentum and build steam as you roll steadily toward the life of your dreams! (Somewhat like a snowball increasing in size until it becomes unstoppable.)

As you feel more content in your life, you positively impact your ability to live peacefully (no fights or hair pulling). This goodwill begins in your community and then ripples around the globe, into the universe and beyond, sending out waves of everlasting joy *(cue Star Wars music)*.

Not only am I a life coach, but I have a quirky sense of humor. I also learned to pat myself on the back because, frankly, waiting for recognition from others can be agonizing. (I'm still waiting, people.)

In my previous life, I was a management consultant for a large company. I doubt they knew I had a sense of humor. I was trying to fit in at the time in my corporate suit—definitely a stretch for a unique character like me.

I use my experience as a management consultant to help people transform their lives, so they feel peaceful, fulfilled, and live authentically. I usually do this with their permission, though occasionally I find myself coaxing people who don't realize they are just longing for a better seat in life!

With a math degree, I think logically and have a knack for solving problems. (Though opening packages still stumps me.) My jobs (typist, computer programmer, consultant, coach, dance teacher, choreographer, dog walker) have all involved sitting down with someone (my boss, an engineer, my client, a wedding couple, a director, or dog owner) to determine their needs. I would then ask questions to be clear about what creative solutions might work for them.

I decided to write a book to impact a wider audience, having experienced terrific success at Life Coaching Magic, coaching clients one-to-one to reach their dreams (often making a big difference in just one session). Please feel free to check out testimonials at www.LifeCoachingMagic.com.

Always fascinated with writing, I wrote my first poem at age 5*. I found humans confusing, and at age 14, I read *I'm OK – You're OK* by Thomas Harris. I thought I had died and gone to heaven. (You mean we can all win? At the same time?) I discovered I enjoyed learning about communication, connection, relationships, self-improvement, and fulfillment. Zillions of books and many personal development courses later, here I stand. Well, actually, here I sit at the keyboard. (What season is it?)

This book is intended to help you change your seat on life's carousel since clearly you have discovered that carousel bench isn't going anywhere close to the brass ring. Venture forth to figure out your life's direction and create your unique journey to achieve your dreams. It is even better if you find yourself laughing a bit along the way.

Kudos to you dear reader — I wish you nothing but the best! I want you to learn the lessons I discovered through books, courses, and life itself. And I'm happy to summarize decades of learning into a shorter form.

So, take a deep breath — wait, breathe already! You've got this. Enjoy discovering secrets that will have life opening up to you.

Here is the poem I wrote at age 5:

> "Bunnies, bunnies everywhere,
> Hopping all around the square
> Come on now and give a cheer,
> For the bunnies of the year."

(Hey, I was 5. What did you expect, Shakespeare? Most impressive is that I've remembered it for decades!)

*"Don't follow your dreams,
run with them!"*

— Dane Cook

OVERVIEW:
YOU CAN HAVE IT ALL

"Life's Magic Carousel: How to Grab the Brass Ring Before the Music Stops"

What if you could live the life that you want today? Try on that idea—because you can.

No, I am not going to grant you three wishes. Hmmm… Well, wait, actually I am.

Think about what those three wishes would be. Hold them in your mind as you read along. Not that I don't trust you, but why not write them down here in case you want to refer to them later:

WISH #1: _____

WISH #2: _____

WISH #3: _____

You have a huge opportunity to change your life.

You may not have been aware of it yet since you didn't go to a fortune-teller.

You can live an amazing life, despite the obstacles that stand in your way (those that are known to you and those that are not). Have patience. Life Coaching Magician Karen will reveal all!

These roadblocks often include common beliefs that you were taught, and continue to live by, even though they are not serving you well. Things like: *You're not enough,* or *you don't matter,* or *you* *should do what everyone else does,* or *telling yourself that was a stupid thing to do.*

You have those three wishes, okay, assuming you wrote them down, which means that your life could be more than it is. (That carousel bench is a bit too familiar, no doubt, and if you want to try and grab the brass ring hanging near the carousel so you win a free ride, you might need to move to another seat closer to the ring!) There are likely things that can be changed easily and quickly, once I show you the obstacles that are blocking your path and keeping you locked into your current life.

These obstacles prevent you from having:

   the life you want
     the life of your dreams
       the life you're afraid to tell people about
         the life that is so freakin' amazing
           the life that would shiver your timbers

So, take this book, wave it high overhead, and let's head into battle! Or just turn the page – that will work, too, though it is far less dramatic.

"If you realize how you can shed your past mistakes as easily as clothing, you could walk boldly into your dream life – that sure would be bold. YIKES! Ok, that image is clearly not what I had in mind."

— Karen Leeds

10 OBSTACLES TO THE MAGICAL LIFE YOU CRAVE

Here are 10 obstacles that keep you locked into your current life and prevent you from having the peaceful, fulfilling, fun life you want. (Keep in mind those three lingering wishes you wrote down that call to you day and night.) You may not have all of the following common obstacles, but if you do, don't worry:

OBSTACLE #1 – TIMING
You believe you can't have the life you want right now. Unfortunately, you think that now is never the right time. *Someday*, you will live your dream life. I get it. But when is someday, exactly?

OBSTACLE #2 – BAGGAGE
You experience guilt or feel unworthy when considering what you want. You don't realize how much baggage you have accumulated. You don't notice this emotional baggage, though others can see it a mile away.

OBSTACLE #3 – ATTITUDE
You might not be aware that <u>you</u> are the biggest obstacle to your dreams. You can probably come up with zillions of reasons why it is not possible to have your dreams. Don't toss your dreams aside like yesterday's garbage.

OBSTACLE #4 – GUILT
You selflessly put others first so you won't feel guilty. I hear you. Rescuing others is typically not helpful to either you or the person you've chosen to rescue unless there's a real emergency.

OBSTACLE #5 – PRIORITY

This may seem like a no-brainer, but it is not enough to be confident in the back row or to fantasize about having a starring role in your own life (though that can be entertaining).

Putting yourself first should not ignore what else is happening. Caregivers should take care of those in their charge, particularly children. There are often ways to delegate certain responsibilities. Consider putting yourself first occasionally. (Geez, are we legally covered now?)

OBSTACLE #6 – BITING YOUR TONGUE

You stay quiet when you're unhappy, even though a part of you desperately wants to say something (and often you are having a raging dialogue in your head).

OBSTACLE #7 – ISOLATION

You believe you are alone and feel disconnected with the flow of life. You often experience life as a struggle in which you are trying desperately to swim upstream. This has not worked so well.

OBSTACLE #8 – FEELING POWERLESS

You believe you have little impact on your life and the lives of others. But you are mistaken.

OBSTACLE #9 – CHOICES

You may not realize the impact of choices you make.

OBSTACLE #10 – INDECISION

Not making a decision is also a choice. It is just a passive, quiet one that slips off into the night with little notice or fanfare.

10 SECRETS FOR CREATING YOUR DREAM LIFE

Here are secrets to battle those pesky obstacles and create your dream life: the life that has been waiting patiently for you to masterfully shape it to an extraordinary fit, as if a tailor had designed it with you in mind - waking up excited to start your day, knowing what you want, discovering relationships are easy and marveling that people actually hear you when you speak.

Here for you and you alone (as well as anyone else reading this book) are these ten bold statements that will alter your destiny. For now, try on the feeling of having the most extraordinary life. And I will give greater detail on these 10:

1. NOW IS THE TIME (NOT LATER)

2. LOSE THE BAGGAGE

3. FEEL CONFIDENT

4. GIVE UP PUTTING OTHERS FIRST

5. PUT YOURSELF FIRST

6. SPEAK UP

7. PARTNER WITH LIFE

8. RECOGNIZE YOUR POWER

9. USE YOUR POWER WISELY

10. CHANGE YOUR SEAT TO GRAB THE BRASS RING

"Life is not a dress rehearsal."

— David Brudnoy

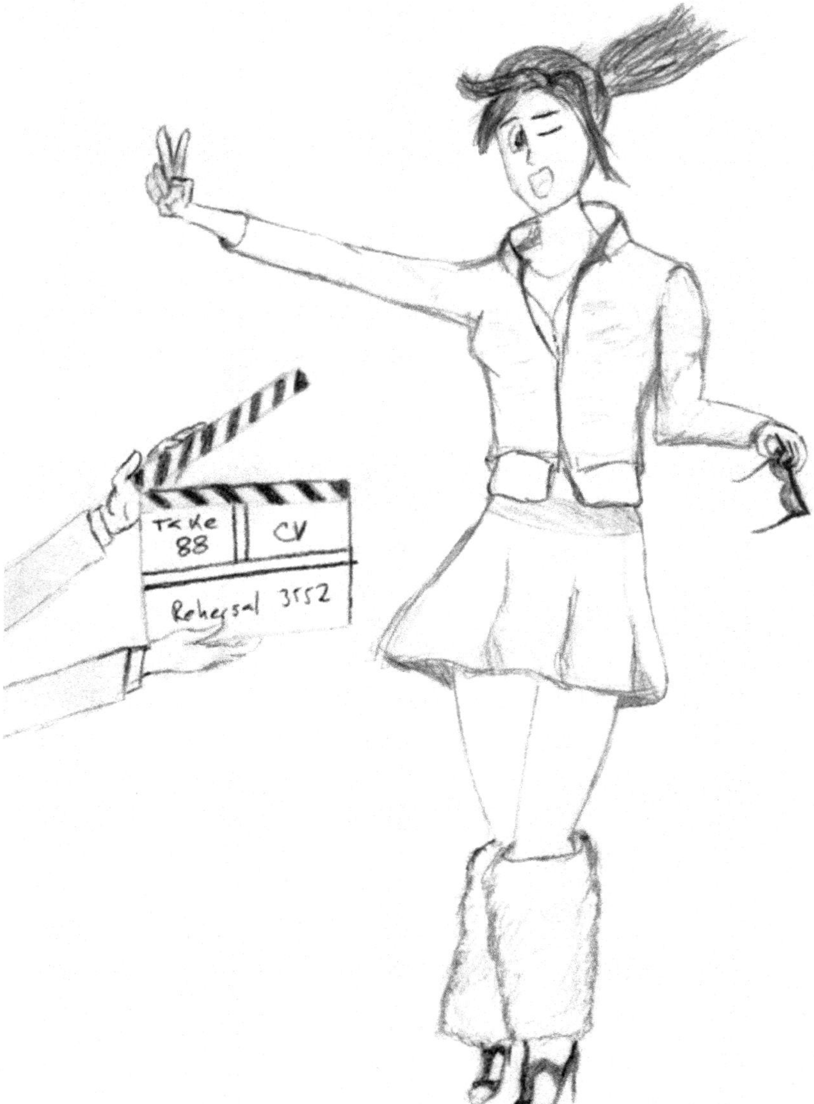
TAKE
88
CV
Rehersal 3552
CV

SECRET #1

NOW IS THE TIME

You believe you can't have the life you want right now. You think that you should just settle, that your life is okay, though you are disappointed and frustrated. You have many reasons why it can't be now. Trust me: there will always be reasons. And the longer you put off having a life that works for you with time and energy to enjoy each moment, the more frustrated and disillusioned you become.

It can be heartbreaking to realize that you have waited too long and will not have the opportunity to make changes. (Hint: It would be best to do this while you are still above ground.) Hey… if you believe in reincarnation and are willing to wait – that's fine. But for the rest of you, the time has come!

If you'd like, you could chant these secrets (like NOW IS THE TIME!) to yourself. Chanting these out loud is not recommended, at least if anyone else is nearby and might look at you oddly (unless one of your life's dreams is to grab negative attention, in which case, I say go for it).

You feel guilty focusing on yourself. You're frazzled trying to put everyone else first – been there, bought that t-shirt. You don't have the time or emotional energy to even think about what you want – and that is just not going to cut it.

You know that what you have right now is not what you wanted when you were young and looked to your future.

Life is OK. Not good or bad, just OK. And if you want to give up on those three wishes and settle for just OK, stay on that carousel bench!

But if you're ready to change seats on life's carousel and grab the brass ring, now is the time.

The horses are traveling magically up and down. They are way more fun than that bench, which is going nowhere fast! I know because I've been there, bench-warming for years, looking around me at those beautiful horses, longing to leave that safe, but predictable, monotonous ride; knowing that, at any moment, I should go for a horse, but instead, biding my time for the perfect moment when the earth might shift and some gravitational force might fling me off the bench and somehow miraculously and carefully settle me onto a fabulous, decorated horse, moving rhythmically up and down. Then, when you are on the moving horse, you can look for the ring. You'll want to position yourself, so that you can reach with one hand and maintain your balance. You will grab a ring and, with hope in your heart, look to see if it is made of brass. It is! You have done it. You have grabbed the brass ring before the music stopped. YEAH YOU!

(Reality check here – Unfortunately, no gravitational force will pluck you off the bench. I know. I waited for years!)

*"I'm one bad relationship away
from having 39 cats."*

— Unknown

SECRET #2

LOSE THE BAGGAGE

You probably don't realize all of the baggage that you have accumulated throughout your life: your fear of spiders, being picked last for sports teams, that scary kid from second grade, your neighbor four doors down, your boss from your last job, and the friend who doesn't bring much to the party.

Baggage can be left over from childhood, relationships, jobs, illness, abuse, etc. It can consist of any of the following.

Check off whether you are carrying any of these types of baggage. (Bonus points if you have all of them and even some that aren't listed here):

_____ low self-esteem (unworthiness)
_____ guilt
_____ worry
_____ hurt
_____ negativity
_____ fear
_____ blame or judgment
_____ sadness
_____ jealousy
_____ shame
_____ grief
_____ anger
_____ hopelessness
_____ desperation
_____ wallowing in self-pity or misery

_____ contemplating becoming a homeless person, wandering life's stage as if you were a character from Shakespeare's *Macbeth*: "What dreams may come when we have shuffled off this mortal coil." (Hold on, that's depressing…)

These feelings give you a negative perspective on life.

Not surprisingly, eliminating these emotions will give you a positive attitude.

Already, you would feel lighter because carrying all of these feelings around creates quite a lot of emotional baggage that you take with you into every relationship and job. You feel snubbed or unappreciated or whatever, from something that happened ages ago. Let it go!

Ok, let's do this in the form of a meditation. Close your eyes if it is safe to do so. (What does that mean anyway?) Take a deep breath. Focus on letting go of the bad stuff.

As you exhale, release all of those bad feelings. They aren't doing you any good. (Hey, don't hyperventilate; we're finally getting to the good stuff.)

If you are having difficulty releasing these feelings, sit down and write a letter to the person who is at the center of these feelings. It can be a way to get rid of these relics that will drag you down…

Writing letters is a great exercise meant for you, not for the person you are addressing.

The whole point of writing the letter is so you can move on.

If you write a letter, do not give it to the person or mail it, even if you are tempted.

You can also write a letter to someone who still upsets you or to someone whom you love and are having difficulty letting go.

You can write a letter to someone who is no longer alive, which can be really helpful because, for crying out loud, how could they have left you like this? Is that fair? Nope—it sure isn't.

Memories are a wonderful thing – both good and bad. I'm not saying erase your past. Just edit out the parts that are keeping you from your destined greatness. Holding on to positive memories is uplifting.

Bad memories actually enable you to learn. But then it is time to MOVE ON!

(The legal department is making me say that if you mail the letter, we cannot be held responsible for what happens next. Legal can be so pushy sometimes…)

If you're stuck, here is a fill-in-the-blank letter to get you started, though it's better to just write whatever comes to mind. Don't hold back.

Dear _____,

I felt really

    a. angry

    b. sad

    c. upset

    d. other _____

when you

    a. called me names

    b. told me I was worthless

    c. ignored me

    d. other _____

I often felt very

    a. unworthy

    b. criticized

    c. unappreciated

    d. other _____

I am now choosing to feel

    a. strong

    b. successful

    c. free

    d. other _____

I have decided to forgive you and move on since I am a great person.

Later!

"If you find yourself in an awkward situation, as I did recently at a dinner party, don't let on. If, after dinner, your chair is so far under the table that you can't push it back when everybody else does, and you feel as helpless as a toddler, act unconcerned and guests will assume you are so fascinated by the conversation that you hadn't noticed the rest of the guests had kicked back."

(Or at least maybe they would be kind and pretend they didn't. Of course, now my friends know, whereas before they had just suspected...)

— Karen Leeds

SECRET #3

BE CONFIDENT

It is easy to be swept along if you aren't confident.

I was swept along for decades. Kind of like a personal tsunami. You never know where you'll wash up and when.

I was painfully shy and walked around looking at the ground for years. That is one reason I started reading about people, relationships, and communication - I felt like I didn't know how to be in this world. I remember being in a play, and when they put me in costume and makeup, nobody knew who I was!

Acting confidently creates respect. Confident people choose a life path that works for them and generates success.

Think about this. If you could wander the world feeling unimportant or you could wander the world confidently, it makes more sense to be confident. Right?

Confidence is a choice.

The only choice
   every time
      for everyone
         even shy people
            even people who never felt confident
            even you.

That's what I'm talking about! I can see it already. You've got that sure smile and that look that says you feel good about who you are. And you should. You are worthy!

Confidence comes from within, though sometimes it appears that certain people are born with it. Pretty annoying, isn't it? How do some people feel confident every step of the friggin' way?

The good news for the other 99% of humanity is that you can start feeling and acting confident at any time, no matter what your life has been like or how many tsunamis have struck. Even hanging onto a pole with your feet flapping.

It is obvious to others whether you are confident by the way you hold yourself, the way you talk and the way you move. Now, keep that image, attitude, and swagger - that's what I'm talkin' about!

Now with that incredibly confident image in mind, check off which of the following apply to you.

Do you walk around with your:

____ Chin up

____ Shoulders back

____ Neck extended

____ Back straight

____ Feet solidly on the ground

____ Attention on the task at hand

____ Eyes connecting with others
(Instead of moving shiftily back and forth)

____ Ready smile
(Watch where you do this. Don't shock anyone)

____ Relaxed breathing

_____ Firm handshake
(Assuming it's appropriate to shake hands)

_____ Easy laugh
(Laughing *with* people, not at them)

_____ Voice strong with nary a quiver
(Unless you are in front of a large angry crowd)

_____ Ability to swallow intact
(As long as scary people aren't around)

_____ Excuses limited to real events
(No "dog ate the homework" kind of thing)

In fact, if you do all of the items in the above checklist and physically adopt the posture of someone who is extremely comfortable in their shoes, remarkably, you will begin to feel confident.

If you are tempted to continue reading without doing this, just take a minute to look in a mirror.

What do you see in the mirror?

I'm not talking about the extra pounds around the middle, the legs that need shaving, the frizzy hair, bony elbows, or anything else that has caught your eye and suddenly needs attention. (Oh – wait. That was all about me – oops!)

Does that face in the mirror look confident?

That voice in your head (saying most of the things you were taught growing up and usually sounding remarkably like one of your parents, siblings, bullies, teachers or bosses) continues to tell you all the reasons you should not be confident.

Boot the voice and replace it with positive commentary.

I call the voice in my head Ewok. He wants to be a friend. This is not, however, something he has had much practice doing. He is not a good friend. (Sorry, Ewok.) Fortunately, the more I ignore him, the quieter he becomes!

Treat this voice like a child.

Encourage positive behavior and pay no attention to insults. (Ewok, I can hear you, but I'm not listening! We talked about this. That's better.)

Or treat it like a stranger – not necessarily welcoming, yet understanding. Polite, yet distant. Patient and accepting, only if Ewok behaves.

It might be odd at first, but that resounding silence can allow your life to become peaceful.

WHAT YOUR EWOK (inner voice or critic) SAYS TO YOU:

_____

_____

_____

_____

_____

Whether or not you are feeling confident – act confidently and you will begin to feel more and more confident.

"I'm sorry.
I can only help one person per day.
Today is not your day.
Tomorrow is not looking good either."

— Unknown

SECRET #4

GIVE UP RESCUING OTHERS

Volunteering and helping others almost always make people happy. It's one of the best things you can do to feel good.

But when you are already stretched to the breaking point, taking on additional responsibilities consumes time and energy and leaves you exhausted and unable to enjoy life.

You might discover that you tend to help people who either don't need your help or could be helped by others.

The goal here is to create balance.

Stop volunteering when you don't need to do so. Let someone else step up to the plate and give them a pat on the back – "Great thing you're doing there, thanks!"

Helping others is fine as long as it isn't creating a burden.

Recently, I found myself helping three women at the same time (a neighbor who had fallen, a mother with legal issues, and a relative needing hand-holding). But the amount of time and energy I spent doing so was completely overwhelming my life! I simply couldn't sustain it and still do all the things I needed to do, let alone have any free time.

By helping others, I wasn't encouraging them to be self-sufficient.

I began to plot and scheme (in the nicest way of course). I figured out how to get each of them to take more responsibility for themselves. And remember, this was also good for them to discover – they did not need to be as dependent upon me as they had been.

I learned that if I didn't respond immediately, they would somehow figure out how to do things – either on their own or by finding some other poor soul to help them.

I didn't stop engaging with them completely, which would have been inconsiderate. In a short period of time, I discovered each one could be fairly self-sufficient.

It's a good feeling to help others. However, the extent to which I had neglected myself was unnecessary.

Also, I appeared to reinforce their belief that they needed someone to lean on and weren't capable of taking care of themselves.

Regaining time and energy can make a world of difference.

Sometimes, you find yourself hanging out with "low dose" people – people that you can only take for a short time.

NAME TEN PEOPLE WITH WHOM YOU WANT TO SPEND LESS TIME:

_____   _____

_____   _____

_____   _____

_____   _____

_____   _____

NAME TEN PEOPLE WITH WHOM YOU WANT TO SPEND MORE TIME:

_____   _____

_____   _____

_____   _____

_____   _____

_____   _____

Here is an example of a coaching client's extraordinary life changes in a very short period of time.

One of my coaching clients was helping a relative. When we met, she told me that she wanted to date, which sounded reasonable to me. I asked her what was currently stopping her from doing that.

My client explained that she had no time and energy. As we spoke, it became clear that she was very willing to pitch in and help others in all walks of life.

Volunteering made her feel good. But it interfered with her life goals. It was time to take a step back.

My client made very few changes. She explained to others that she wasn't going to be able to continue to help at the same level. This was important to communicate, so that they wouldn't feel abandoned.

In addition, as she thought about the possibility of dating, she realized that her living situation was uncomfortable and would not give her any privacy, even on the phone.

She decided to move and gave up some time demands. She also

quickly began to recharge now that she had space and time to just breathe.

Once she removed these two major constraints, she had time and energy to date!

"Give a man a fish;
You have fed him for today.
Teach a man to fish;
You have fed him for a lifetime."

— Unknown

SECRET #5

PUT YOURSELF FIRST

You probably feel guilty, selfish, greedy, and mean when you consider putting yourself first.

For decades, I was quiet and lived life in the shadows, like my mother did for the most part.

Unfortunately, our society and community taught many (often women) to take a back seat to other people's needs:

I will never forget boarding a plane and watching my mom as she got up to put her coat into the overhead bin. She couldn't open the compartment without stepping further into the aisle. She didn't feel that it was her "place" to do that.

Instead, my mom awkwardly smiled and nodded at people, pretending she didn't mind and waited in an uncomfortable half standing position for 10 minutes! Once everyone had boarded the plane, she was able to step into the aisle and put her coat in the overhead compartment. Only then was she finally able to sit down.

Step forward and claim your spot in the sun (or your section of the aisle in this case).

Other passengers clearly expected my mom to put up her coat and would have likely waited a few seconds.

If you are very shy or quiet, you may have to aim for being a bit more assertive than feels comfortable for you in order to be heard.

I'm not suggesting being rude (rarely a good idea).

Doing what anybody else would do makes sense and brings you peace.

(It also causes less of a backache – those compartments are really low so you can't fully stand up...)

LIST THREE SITUATIONS OR RELATIONSHIPS IN WHICH YOU WILL BEGIN TO PUT YOURSELF FIRST (at least occasionally):

#1 _____

_____

#2 _____

_____

#3 _____

_____

*"It's easier to speak up
once you stop biting your tongue."*

—Karen Leeds

SECRET #6

SPEAK UP

Were you taught not to answer back as a child? Most people cringe when they consider speaking up. Did you know:

Research has found people fear public speaking more than death!

I'm not suggesting you take up public speaking in front of a large audience. Speaking up to one person is definitely easier.

Most of us have experience with people who speak up in an aggressive manner.

Their style of speaking up is not only inappropriate, but often isn't successful. (No surprise, these are the people who have had confidence to spare since birth. How did this happen?)

It is not necessary to speak up in a surly, rude manner. You can say what is on your mind in a polite way. Humor often works well, too.

Here is a list of situations you might find yourself in. Feel free to develop your own list, or you can use mine, as long as you give it back. Hey, I'm watching you!

You might find some of the following situations fairly comfortable while others would cause nervousness, sweaty palms, and hyperventilating. Wait—are you okay there?

PICTURE YOURSELF IN THE FOLLOWING SITUATIONS TO PRACTICE SPEAKING UP.

Location #1: Grocery Store (great place to speak up!)

Situation: Your mouth-watering lasagna has no rubber band, and it might ooze onto the rest of your groceries.

Say: **"Could you please put a rubber band on that?"**

(Bonus: "Last time my lasagna spilled all over.")

Location #2: Restaurant (don't blame me if you keep quiet)

Situation: You ordered a rare steak, but it arrives well-done.

Say: **"Could you please bring me a rare steak as I ordered?"**

(Bonus: "This puppy looks like shoe leather.")

Location #3: Zoo (Ever notice how often animals speak up?)

Situation: You are given incorrect change and refuse to head to the monkey house until corrected.

Say: **"Excuse me. I was given incorrect change."**

(Bonus: "At this rate, I'd be paying $2 per monkey — must be some pretty amazing critters.")

Location #4: Friend's house (be honest with your buddy)

Situation: Your friend asks for a second favor this week.

Say: **"I'm sorry. I wish I could help you."**

(Note: Give no reason, just shake your head no.)

Location #5: Movie theater (movie choice is key)

Situation: You are the only one in the group who has no interest in seeing a horror movie.

Say: **"I don't like scary movies. Let's see this one instead."**

(Note: If they won't budge, you can probably find a more thoughtful group of "friends.")

Location #6: Family reunion (try not to step on many egos)

Situation: Your uncle makes fun of your pointy ears.

Say: **"That comment hurts my feelings."**

(Note: Refrain from mentioning his big nose.)

Location #7: On a date (tricky if you can't speak up here)

Situation: You discover you would rather go home early to wash your cat.

Say: **"I'm sorry. I need to go home now."**

(Note: You don't need to explain why. I probably wouldn't mention the cat...)

Location #8: Meeting presentation (need to speak up here)

Situation: You discover your presentation was attacked with a crayon by your niece.

Say: **"I think the gremlins offered their ideas on this!"**

<u>Location #9</u>: Relative's house (tread gently with this bunch)

<u>Situation</u>: Your mother-in-law asks you a question that you'd rather not answer since it is out of line.

Say: **"I'm sorry, that question makes me feel uncomfortable."**

(Note: I wouldn't add that she often makes you uncomfortable.)

<u>Location #10</u>: Shopping mall (your home away from home)

<u>Situation</u>: Your friend says something embarrassing in a really loud voice.

Say: **"I think a few people in the corner missed that."**

(Note: Laugh with people, not at them.)

That wasn't so bad, was it?

Like exercising, speaking up builds that muscle. Every time you say what is on your mind, it becomes easier.

Start with low-key situations first and work your way up to more intense scenarios. This desensitization technique is often used to decrease anxiety – not that you tend to get nervous. Oh no, not you.

As long as you speak up with kindness and without blame or judgment, you will be seen as confident. Start to notice others' reactions.

Many times, it is more appropriate and caring to speak up rather than to remain silent.

"It's great to find that one special person you want to annoy for the rest of your life."

— Rita Rudner

SECRET #7

PARTNER WITH LIFE

All of us have partners, whether we are in relationships with parents, kids, bosses, etc. **I believe there is also a way to "partner with life."**

As a dance teacher and choreographer, I learned that a successful dance partnership does not just happen. I have danced socially with many different partners and discovered there are a few ingredients to a great partnership.

As a life coach, I became intrigued by the idea of "dancing" through life.

If you adapt approaches that work for dance couples, you will become very good at "partnering" with life.

You are more likely to achieve your goals when working cooperatively with life. (No surprise, eh?)

Many people act passively year after year and then are unhappy with where they end up.

An ability to apply the following ten dance techniques when you partner with life will enable you to move effortlessly.

1 – CHOOSE TO LEAD

In dance, a couple must choose a leader. Only one can lead. If you don't lead, the alternative is to be a follower. In life, if you don't lead, then others will influence your direction. As time slips by, you might not be happy if you haven't ticked off a single item on your wishlist. (And don't come crawling to me if that happens.)

Ideally, you would choose to lead and take charge of your direction in life.

2 - SELECT A SPEED OR RHYTHM (that works for you)

The rhythm of your music creates overall structure for your dance. Some people rush through life at a breakneck pace, which can be dizzying for the rest of us. Allowing breathing time can both reduce stress and empower you.

If you find the rhythm of your life isn't working for you, change the pace. You can slow your speed: take on fewer activities, knock items off your to-do list, and pursue what is meaningful to you.

3 - LISTEN TO THE MUSIC (tune in to your heart)

If the music is too quiet, it may be difficult to dance in time to its rhythm. In life, you may discover that you can no longer hear the music in your heart. Perhaps your job isn't a fit. Maybe you want to create your own company or follow a unique path in life.

In life, stop and listen carefully to the music you hear in your heart. Only by honoring what speaks to you can you feel truly fulfilled.

4 - CREATE RESPECT AND TRUST

When leading a dance, it is fine to be assertive, but not aggressive. Heavy-handedness in dance is uncomfortable and ineffective. In life, aggression creates resistance and interferes with communication, like static.

Awareness, sensitivity, respect, and trust are valuable keys to success. Be someone with whom you would like to partner.

5 - PLAN YOUR PATH (but keep it flexible)

In dance, how you get to your destination is called floorcraft. Running over people is just as unforgivable in life as it is on the dance floor.

Remain flexible, make changes in direction, and allow for more time when possible.

6 - PHYSICALLY RELAX

The tension in your body impacts everything you do, creating stress and eroding the connection with your dance partner. Sometimes in life, you only discover you are tense when you try to relax. (Neck pain is a good indicator, too.)

Tension interferes with communication and is always obvious to others.

7 - NOTICE NON-VERBAL CUES

Only 7% of communication is based on words. On the dance floor, a follower may touch a leader's shoulder to indicate that he needs to dance in place for a few beats to avoid a collision with another couple. In life, much is communicated by body language and tone of voice. If you are acting inappropriately, you might get a raised eyebrow. (Uh-oh, not the raised eyebrow!)

People pay greater attention to tone and body language when they contradict the words you are saying.

Real life example: I knew someone who made people nervous, even though he was smiling. He confessed to me that he would say nasty things in his head. He thought others didn't notice, but people felt uneasy and confused by him. People experienced his manner as untrustworthy - the look in his eyes came across loud and clear.

8 - WEAR SHOES YOU CAN TURN IN (have good support)

Your attire and choices can easily work against you. Wearing high heels when dancing a fast hustle may throw you off center. The life choices you make in your workspace, relationships, community, and home should work for you.

Create as much opportunity for success as possible.

9 - FOCUS ON THE JOURNEY (keep it flexible)

Noticing your partner is off balance is a good way to avoid catastrophe on the dance floor. In life, generosity and goodwill create a team mentality and connection, keeping you on track.

People respond best when you are generous, understand their needs, and can anticipate them. Remember that the journey is often as important as the destination and may ultimately help you shift in order to get there.

10 - SMILE WHATEVER HAPPENS (keep a sense of perspective)

Mistakes are often missed if dancers are smiling and enjoying themselves. Stop taking yourself so seriously. If you aren't smiling, try a different dance, a new partner, or wait for a slower song. (Otherwise, you're a real drag.)

If you can't laugh at yourself, it's time to make changes.

"A computer once beat me at chess, but it was no match for me at kickboxing."

—Stelian Pilici

SECRET #8

RECOGNIZE YOUR POWER

You might be unaware that often YOU are the biggest obstacle to your dreams. (Sorry to break it to you...)

Like most, you probably believe your life is set in stone.

It often appears that way, but you have complete control.

You can choose the direction you want for your life.

You may not realize just how easy it is to change your life.

Recognizing your power and then using it to move in the direction you choose makes your journey easier.

Here are eight key steps to first recognizing, and then stepping into, your power.

Consider whether you do any or all of the following eight Key Elements of Power:

1 - DO YOU TRUST YOUR INTUITION?   _____

Take time to tune into your feelings and what your heart is suggesting you should do.

Trust your instincts and inner gut reactions to people and situations. Pay attention if you feel nervous, even if you're not sure why.

2 - DO YOU KNOW WHAT MOTIVATES YOU?   _____

Are you more of a team player, or do you prefer to be independent? Are you happy to plod along so that life is peaceful, or are you going for recognition? Is it competition, achievement, group effort, mentoring a younger person, making money, making a difference, or teaching others that inspires you?

Figure out what drives you and put that front and center in your life.

3 - DO YOU ACT LIKE A ROLE MODEL?   _____

Others involved in your journey may be looking to you for guidance. Acting like a role model keeps you, your decisions, and your moves positive and appropriate for a healthy, rewarding path.

Create a positive impression.

4 - DO YOU GAIN SUPPORT FROM OTHERS?   _____

Keep your radar tuned to others' feelings. Having others on your side or team can make a tremendous difference.

Try to pick up on the emotion of others before you blindly barge ahead with your agenda.

5 - DO YOU RESPOND EFFECTIVELY? _____

Have a variety of moves in your tool kit. Asking a thoughtful question instead of criticizing allows others to change their approach without losing face.

People respond well to optimism, positivity, warmth, compassion, humor, acceptance, and kindness.

6 - DO YOU GIVE ADVANCE NOTICE? _____

Signal your intent for greater power and effectiveness. Catching others unaware isn't desirable.

Knowing what is coming keeps others calm and ready to move.

7 - DO YOU PROJECT A SUCCESSFUL IMAGE? _____

What you wear, the way you feel about yourself, the way you move, and whether you're looking for approval all make a difference.

The unique way you see and believe in yourself has the most impact on your image.

8 - DO YOU CREATE A NO BLAME ZONE? _____

Blaming is ineffective, negative, and a waste of time. Looking to assign blame undermines your effectiveness and diminishes the respect you receive from others.

Learn from what happened, make appropriate changes, and move on peacefully without pointing fingers.

"You're only given a little spark of madness. You mustn't lose it."

— Robin Williams

SECRET #9

USE YOUR POWER WISELY

The following true story indicates a very important point.

People easily and unknowingly give up their power to create the outcome they want.

See if you can pick up on how Mr. Speed Dating actually "creates" an outcome that will make him unhappy.

Years ago, I went to a speed-dating event. A middle-aged guy sat down across from me. His shirt was covered with crumbs, and he was completely unaware of it.

I opened my mouth to say something (as a favor to him), but before I could say a word, he interrupted me.

"I can't believe it. I am so disappointed with the women at this event. They aren't particularly attractive. They don't know how to present themselves. They don't have anything interesting to say. What on earth are they thinking?"

I paused for a second, smiled, and shook my head. I was not sure how to respond, though I was tempted to pull out a mirror. This might actually be the point at which I decided to become a life coach.

"I hear you," I finally reply.

He continued, *"Honestly, how can anyone believe they would be considered attractive to the opposite sex if they didn't put their best foot forward for that critical first impression? Speaking for myself, negative comments would certainly not make me want to willingly talk with someone again."*

Notice how he displayed all the elements that he didn't like in the women he was meeting.

I decided that maybe he wouldn't be very receptive to feedback from me. (Ya think?)

As I got up, he started the same conversation with the next woman. I might be wrong, but I suspect he didn't end up with any matches.

Did he have any idea the impact he had on that outcome?

"All human unhappiness is caused by unmet expectations."

—Buddha

SECRET #10

CHANGE YOUR CAROUSEL SEAT (TO GRAB THE BRASS RING)

According to the Buddha, our dreams create expectations for our lives, and if we don't meet those expectations, we will be unhappy.

Be determined to change your seat on life's carousel, so that you meet your life's expectations and are happy.

Since that bench is not getting you where you want to go, you will find yourself eyeing one of the horses that is closer to the ring.

Choose a horse on the outside for the ride you want in life.

Here are five tactics to change seats on life's carousel:

Tactic #1 – DECIDE ON YOUR DESTINATION
Picture your dream in your mind

Tactic #2 – DETERMINE THE BEST PATH
Figure out how to get there (which may involve research)

Tactic #3 – COMMIT TO THIS GOAL
Decide you will make it happen

Tactic #4 – GET EXCITED AND GAIN SUPPORT
Talk it up to everyone and accept help from others

Tactic #5 – GO
Take the first real step

TACTIC #1 – DECIDE ON YOUR DESTINATION

What do you want out of life? Picture your dream in your mind.

Figuring out your goals helps determine your destination.

You may have several possible destinations. (You can always toss a coin if you're deciding among several.)

What three goals (or destinations) do you want to achieve?

For example:

- *create five hours for myself each week*
- *find a less stressful job*
- *heal the relationship with my mom*

YOUR TURN—WHAT THREE GOALS DO YOU WANT TO REACH:

#1 _____

#2 _____

#3 _____

CHOOSE TO FOCUS ON ONE GOAL/DESTINATION FOR NOW:

(Example: I choose to heal the relationship with my mom.)

_____

Keep an open mind. Have you ever traveled and discovered something spectacular on the way to where you were initially headed?

Know that you can change your mind and switch destinations at any time.

TACTIC #2 – DETERMINE THE BEST PATH

Now, consider several paths to get to your goal (this may involve research).

Some paths are more efficient than others and will get you to your destination sooner. (But maybe getting there quickly isn't important.)

Now that you've identified your goal/destination, list three possible ways to get there (or paths):

Example: To heal my relationship with my mom: 1) My mom and I could see a therapist, 2) I could write her a letter, or 3) the two of us could spend a fun day together.

LIST THREE POSSIBLE PATHS TO YOUR GOAL:

#1 _____

#2 _____

#3 _____

Now, choose the path that will get you there and that is best suited to you. *[Example: I want to spend a fun day with my mom at a beach and then walk around the boardwalk at night.]*

YOUR CHOSEN PATH/DIRECTION:

_____

_____

_____

(Relax, you don't need to get there today!)

TACTIC #3 – COMMIT TO THIS GOAL

Decide that you will take this path.

If you commit to this journey, then your attitude and motivation start to impact your life.

You began thinking about where you wanted to go. You researched and learned what this journey involves. Your perspective and thinking move you along, even before you have taken any real steps toward your goal.

Example: Now that you're thinking about a day with your mom, you discover while watching the local news that there is a festival this weekend in a neighboring town that might be even better than what you had considered.

WHAT WILL YOU DO TO COMMIT TO YOUR DREAM?

_____

_____

_____

_____

_____

_____

_____

_____

TACTIC #4 – BECOME EXCITED AND GAIN SUPPORT

Once you begin to try on this destination and picture this journey really happening, talk it up to everyone and get their support. When you put out to the world where you are headed, you'll find assistance in your journey (even when you don't directly ask for it; it's almost uncanny how this happens).

Watch the universe throw support your way.

An example of how talking about your goal changes things:

Recently, a woman in my class mentioned a type of career she had considered, and a few hours later, I ran into someone who would be a perfect source of information for her in that venture. Her mentioning it brought it into my field of awareness. Otherwise, I would not have paid particular attention to that comment and I would not have found an ideal person for my classmate to meet.

Having friends, family, classmates, neighbors, co-workers, and your community on board to give you emotional support and information speeds up the process.

[Example: I will find support for my direction by doing three things: 1) ask dad for ideas, 2) ask my mom's friend what she might enjoy, and 3) check the local paper for events.]

LIST SUPPORTS THAT YOU CAN LEAN ON:

#1 _____

#2 _____

#3 _____

TACTIC #5 – GO

Take the first real step.

You know your destination and the path you've chosen to get there. You got excited about your dream and accepted support from others.

Now, it's time to take that first step. (You can do it!)

Sometimes, taking the first step is difficult. But that first step starts the process moving, and from there, it is like a ball rolling downhill. As it travels, it gathers speed and becomes unstoppable. Uh-oh - look out!

You will discover that with each small step in the process, you have created momentum, and each next step becomes easier than the one before.

Taking these steps in order will enable you to achieve your dream:

- **Picture your dream in your mind**
- **Research how to get there**
- **Commit to one possibility (decide it will happen)**
- **Emotionally accept this vision (get excited about it) and rely on the support of others (your peeps)**
- **Take the first big step**

It may seem difficult in the beginning if the destination is far away.

Remember Dorothy and the yellow brick road? She made it to Oz, so that she could find her way back home.

DOROTHY'S JOURNEY HOME

Dorothy would have been miserable if she didn't get home. (Remember — all human unhappiness is caused by unmet expectations, and getting back to Kansas was her goal.)

She wanted to go home (since there was no place like it).

Dorothy asked everyone she saw and decided to take the yellow brick road to Oz to talk to the Wizard (since, after all, he could do anything).

She told everyone along the way what she wanted, and she relied on support from many others including:

- munchkins
- Glinda the Good Witch
- the Scarecrow
- the Tin Man
- the Cowardly Lion

She stayed on her path, even in the face of obstacles such as:

- fields of poppies
- flying monkeys
- the Wicked Witch of the West

Dorothy followed the yellow brick road (while singing "We're Off to See the Wizard" to keep up her courage for the journey). She finally knocked on the big gate of Oz so that she could find her way back home.

And once in Oz, Dorothy even pulled aside the big curtain, though she was afraid of the loud voice. (That's the way!)

PROCESS FOR CHANGING CAROUSEL SEATS

Here is an example closer to earth. Say someone is sitting on the bench of life's carousel and wanting to change seats since that bench is not moving and is nowhere near the brass ring!

DESTINATION – The blue horse that moves up and down

PATH – It is easier to walk three horses in front of you than 16 behind you (remember the carousel is still moving folks)

COMMIT – Picture the new exciting ride you'll get

RELY ON SUPPORT – The person next to you notices you starting to rise and offers you a hand getting up

TAKE THE FIRST STEP – You get up off that bench and walk to that blue moving carousel horse!

Wait until that carousel stops turning
   I do not recommend switching seats in mid-ride
      Hey that's really dangerous
         Watch it, you might get hurt
            Oh, for crying out loud

[Legal – what do we do now? Are we liable?]

HOW TO GRAB THE BRASS RING ONCE ON A MOVING HORSE

You are now on a moving horse. Congratulations!

Now, you might ask, how the heck do I grab a brass ring?

It is actually the same process we just went through.

DESTINATION – You want to grab the brass ring, so you first look where the rings are dispensed. (Ah, they are attached to that tree branch.)

PATH – You notice the rhythm other riders are using, so you are aware when is the best time to reach out.

COMMIT – You hold onto your beautiful, moving horse with one hand so you are steady and won't fall off (careful now).

RELY ON SUPPORT – Your friends are cheering you on and shouting advice to reinforce when to reach for it, so you actually pull a ring instead of just scraping your knuckles.

TAKE THE FIRST STEP – You go for it and grab. Yes – you did it – you got the brass ring!

"Become the hero of your own life story."

— David Howitt

WHAT STANDS IN YOUR WAY ARE FOUR MAIN OBSTACLES!

(Sorry, that's the largest type they had.)

Obstacle #1:

The myth that life is set in stone

Obstacle #2:

Your death grip on the familiar

Obstacle #3:

Your focus on past mistakes

Obstacle #4:

Those voices in your head

SUMMARY OF KEY POINTS

❖ **You are worthy of having a remarkable life.**

❖ **You can begin to have the life you want right now.**

❖ **More than anything else, the following are what stand in your way:**

- Your mistaken belief that life is set in stone and is difficult to change

- Your death grip on the familiar (not really comfortable, yet known to you)

- Your unwillingness to move beyond your past mistakes and forgive yourself and others

- Your fascination with the voices in your head which cause guilt, worry, fear, and anger

❖ **You can change your life quickly and easily if you choose to do so and walk into your dream life now.**

❖ **YOU CAN CHANGE YOUR SEAT ON LIFE'S CAROUSEL**

❖ **THAT BENCH ISN'T GOING ANYWHERE.**

❖ **YOU CAN GET TO A MOVING HORSE.**

❖ **DECIDE TO CHANGE YOUR SEAT AND GRAB THE BRASS RING!**

LIST OF STRAIGHTFORWARD SECRETS

❖ NOW IS THE TIME
(not someday)

❖ LOSE THE BAGGAGE
(feelings like guilt or sadness; letter writing can help)

❖ BE CONFIDENT
(believe, stand straight, eject Ewok - the voice in your head)

❖ GIVE UP RESCUING OTHERS
(allow other adults to be self-sufficient)

❖ PUT YOURSELF FIRST
(you only get one life – make it your dream life)

❖ SPEAK UP
(start slowly – begin speaking up when you are experiencing physical or emotional discomfort)

DETAIL OF MOST POWERFUL SECRETS

PARTNER WITH LIFE (lessons from partner dancing)

- ❖ CHOOSE TO LEAD

- ❖ SELECT A SPEED OR RHYTHM

- ❖ LISTEN TO YOUR MUSIC

- ❖ CREATE RESPECT AND TRUST

- ❖ PLAN YOUR FLEXIBLE PATH

- ❖ PHYSICALLY RELAX

- ❖ NOTICE NON-VERBAL CUES

- ❖ WEAR SHOES YOU CAN TURN IN
  (so your life fits and won't trip you – life doesn't want you
  to be a klutz)

- ❖ FOCUS ON THE JOURNEY

- ❖ SMILE WHATEVER HAPPENS
  (unless embarrassed for some reason, in which case
  sheepishness is ok)

RECOGNIZE YOUR POWER

❖ TRUST YOUR INTUITION

❖ KNOW WHAT MOTIVATES YOU

❖ ACT LIKE A ROLE MODEL

❖ GAIN SUPPORT FROM OTHERS

❖ RESPOND EFFECTIVELY

❖ GIVE ADVANCE NOTICE
   (don't surprise others)

❖ PROJECT A SUCCESSFUL IMAGE

❖ CREATE A NO-BLAME ZONE

❖ MINIMIZE YOUR DESTRUCTIVE POWER
   (OR use your power for good, not evil)

CHANGE YOUR SEAT TO GRAB THE BRASS RING

❖ DECIDE ON YOUR DESTINATION
   (picture your dream in your mind)

❖ DETERMINE THE BEST PATH TO GET THERE
   (the best path for you)

❖ COMMIT TO THIS GOAL
   (embrace it with all its warts)

❖ BECOME EXCITED AND GAIN SUPPORT
   (take what the universe sends your way)

❖ GO!
   (take that first big step)

POCKET GUIDE

(Who, What, When, Where, Why, and How)

If you don't want to carry the book around (I'll try not to feel too hurt), you could remember the main points using one of two ways. You could refer to this pocket guide below, or the humorous short, sloped story on the next page.

First, you could ask yourself the typical six questions:

<u>WHO</u> – YOU (the main obstacle)

<u>WHAT</u> – BAGGAGE (guilt, worry, jealousy, anger, past issues)

<u>WHEN</u> – NOW (don't wait, someday may never come)

<u>WHERE</u> – JOURNEY (small steps in the direction of your goal are fine)

<u>WHY</u> – WORTHY (you deserve your dream life - on the carousel horses and aiming to grab that brass ring!)

<u>HOW</u> – These are actually the five stages to set yourself in motion once you've got your perspective tweaked (one last review):

- Destination – determine your target
- Direction – which way to head
- Tilt – try it on and figure out what's involved
- Support – allow others to help you
- Go – take that first step

HUMOROUS STORY FOR SECRETS

Try this humorous, visually sloped short story for remembering the key secrets:

YOU
pack your BAGGAGE
into a suitcase. NOW
you hear and eject that VOICE.
Go through the door CONFIDENTLY.
On the way to your DESTINATION
knowing your DIRECTION
you GIVE UP RESCUING OTHERS
that you see on the side of the road. You TILT
for the airport. Others offer to you their SUPPORT.
Of all the passengers you discover that you are FIRST
to board the plane. You RECOGNIZE YOUR POWER
to your seatmate - wanting the window seat you SPEAK UP.
As you exchange seats with him you nod at the clouds to
acknowledge your PARTNER LIFE.
You've CHOSEN YOUR SEAT on life's magic carousel
and you are near the rings.
You decide the right time is NOW
for you to leave the BENCH.
You walk and take your SEAT
on the moving and exciting blue HORSE.
You reach and grab a ring – it is BRASS!
You now have an extraordinary life!
That's right. You did it!
Way to go!!!
YEAH!

~~~~

To Schedule a

60 Minute 1:1

Coaching Session,

Contact

Karen@LifeCoachingMagic.com

with COACHING in subject line

*Bring your dreams to earth
while you are still here to enjoy them!*

Look for two more books coming January 2023:

1) GET OUT OF YOUR OWN WAY

20 Secrets to Stop Being the Biggest Obstacle
10 Ways to Tap into Your Subconscious and
Get the Universe on Your Side

2) SPEAK SO PEOPLE HEAR YOU

7 Ways People Are Different that Matter
14 Little-Known Communication Secrets

Made in USA - Kendallville, IN
76618_9780996906906
08 24 2022 1641